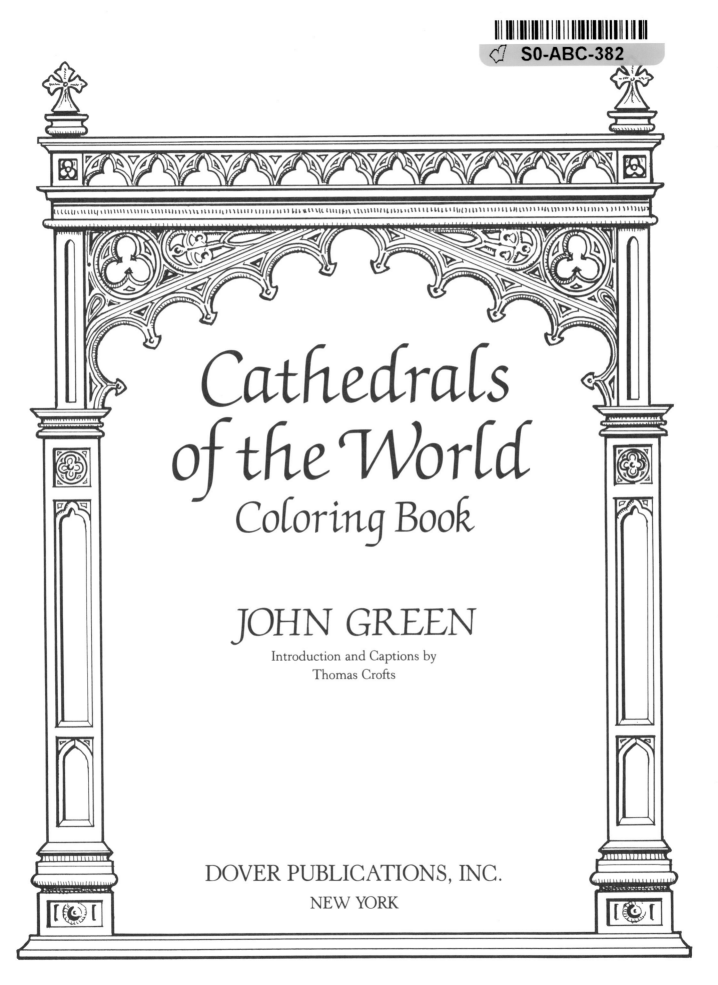

Cathedrals of the World
Coloring Book

JOHN GREEN

Introduction and Captions by
Thomas Crofts

DOVER PUBLICATIONS, INC.

NEW YORK

Hagia Sophia, Istanbul.

Monument to Hugues Libergier (died 1263), a
noted Gothic architect, at Reims Cathedral. He
is shown with the tools of the architect: measuring rod, set square and calipers. For more about
the cathedral at Reims, turn to page 18.

Cathedral of Brasília, Brazil.

Copyright

Illustrations copyright © 1994 by John Green.
Text copyright © 1994 by Dover Publications, Inc.
All rights reserved under Pan American and International Copyright
Conventions.

Published in Canada by General Publishing Company, Ltd., 30 Lesmill Road,
Don Mills, Toronto, Ontario.

Bibliographical Note

Cathedrals of the World Coloring Book is a new work, first published by Dover
Publications, Inc., in 1994.

DOVER *Pictorial Archive* SERIES

This book belongs to the Dover Pictorial Archive Series. You may use the
designs and illustrations for graphics and crafts applications, free and without
special permission, provided that you include no more than four in the same
publication or project. (For permission for additional use, please write to:
Permissions Department, Dover Publications, Inc., 180 Varick Street, New York,
N.Y. 10014.)

However, republication or reproduction of any illustration by any other
graphic service, whether it be in a book or in any other design resource, is strictly
prohibited.

International Standard Book Number: 0-486-28339-9

Manufactured in the United States of America
Dover Publications, Inc., 31 East 2nd Street, Mineola, N.Y. 11501

INTRODUCTION

Traditionally the seat of a bishop and the principal church of a diocese, a cathedral is a monumental fixture in a town- or cityscape, lending unity to all places from which its spires are visible, or its bells audible. Though not every church nowadays referred to as a cathedral is the seat of a bishop, all are buildings that aspire to a transcendent beauty and tranquillity, raised by architects who have attempted to express, in earthly terms, some notion of the heavenly.

The cathedrals rendered for coloring in this book span virtually the entire course of Christian church-building, beginning with the grandest of Byzantine churches: Hagia Sophia (532–537 A.D.). Based on the principles of classical Greek and Roman building, Byzantine architecture made the contribution of the pendentive support, whereby massive structures (in this case domes) could be supported by a system of arches, a technique without which the elaborately conceived roof of Hagia Sophia would have been impossible.

Following the Byzantine, in the early 11th century, was the Romanesque style, which, also influenced by Roman architecture, stressed the rounded arch and the ceiling vault (vaults covered space using the principle of the arch on a three-dimensional basis). It was the modification of the arch and the vault that brought about the style known as Gothic, which began around the mid-12th century. Arches became pointed, interiors loftier and windows much larger; and the development of ribbed vaulting gave new textures to vaulted surfaces, which were now much larger as well. In general, the Gothic is marked by an absence of classical influence, an elaborateness of decoration and an emotionalism that ranges from the serene to the ecstatic, sometimes verging on the hysterical. It was in this period that cathedral-building became almost a craze throughout Europe: in the Middle Ages labor was cheap, and bishops were very powerful; and even the smallest diocese desired the distinction of a great church. The fortunate combination of these influences and the strides then being made in architecture and engineering has left us with some of the most sublime monuments in the history of Western art.

When the Renaissance came, in the 15th and 16th centuries, the classical virtues of symmetry, balance and reason were rediscovered. St. Peter's Basilica in Rome suggests, however, that building on a spectacular (even exaggerated) scale and direct appeal to the spirit were not eschewed in the Renaissance. The Baroque period (early 17th to late 18th centuries), which is generally known for its dense ornamentation (the word baroque is often used synonymously with excess and decadence), began in some parts of Europe as a more austere, even ascetic movement, to which the Spanish and Spanish colonial architecture of the early part of this period can bear witness. Of course, within the Baroque, as within every classification, there are various currents, local and international, as well as aberrations of every sort, which thwart generalization and keep art interesting. The examples of modern architecture represented in the present volume, which range from Gothic Revival to Art Nouveau to Post-modern, demonstrate that church-building remains a vigorous art, thriving on experimentation as well as notions of the heavenly.

The cathedrals are presented here in chronological order, generally based on the date their construction began; in the case of churches repeatedly built, the date of the most recent construction is used. The magnificent cathedral of Notre Dame in Paris has been placed slightly out of chronological order so that it might occupy the centerfold of this book.

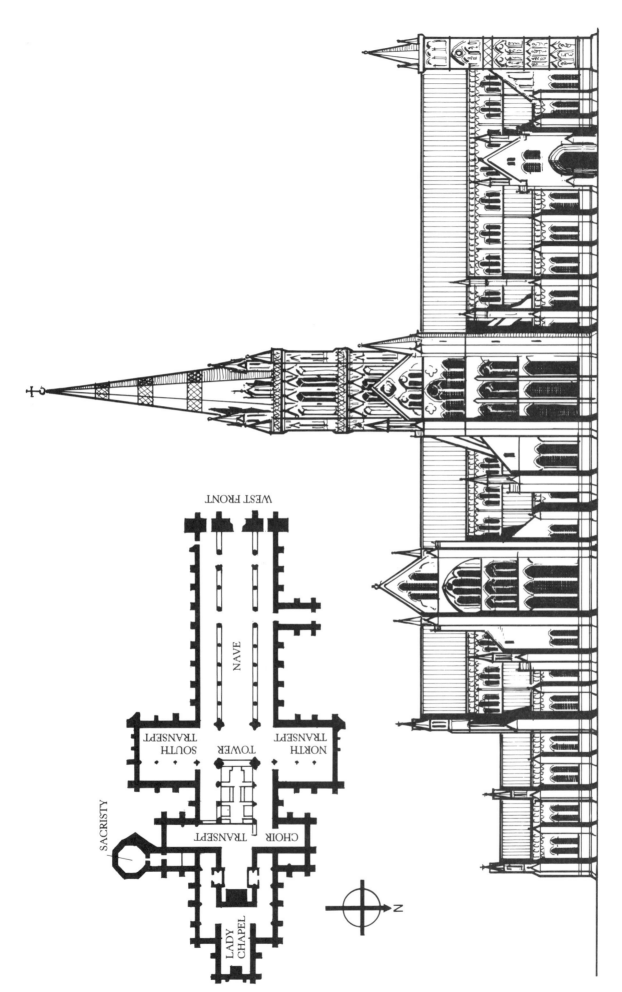

Ground plan and elevation of a Gothic cathedral. This is Salisbury Cathedral in England. The ground plans of Gothic cathedrals are generally in the shape of a cross, though the style of the cross often varies.

The elevation shows the vertical dimensions of a building. For another view of Salisbury Cathedral and more about its construction, turn to page 27.

WEST FRONT

NAVE

SOUTH TRANSEPT

TOWER

NORTH TRANSEPT

SACRISTY

CHOIR TRANSEPT

LADY CHAPEL

N

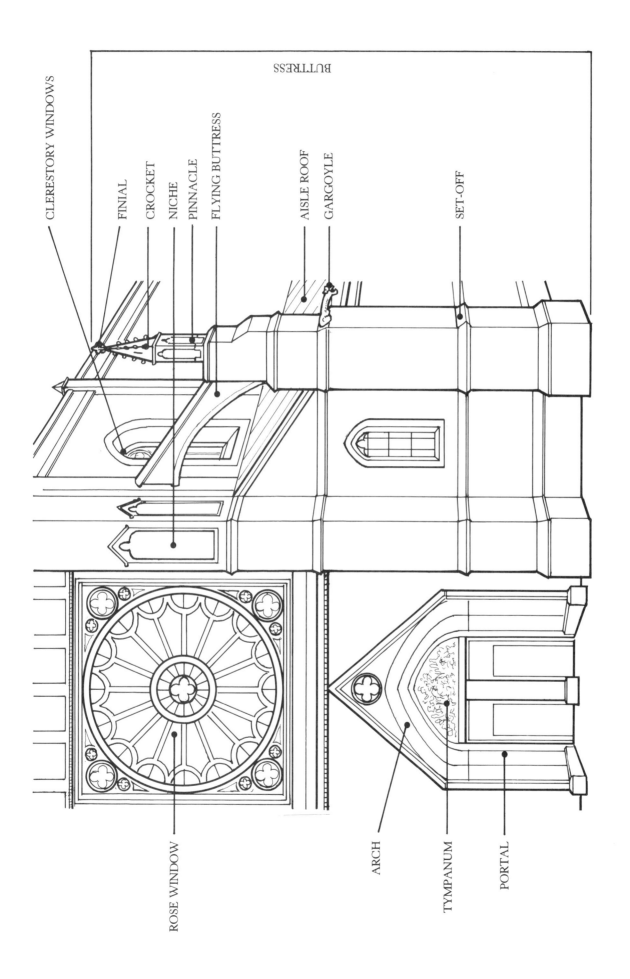

CLERESTORY WINDOWS

FINIAL
CROCKET
NICHE
PINNACLE
FLYING BUTTRESS

AISLE ROOF
GARGOYLE

BUTTRESS

SET-OFF

ROSE WINDOW

ARCH

TYMPANUM

PORTAL

Elements of the Gothic. In this diagram, which features an exterior view of a cathedral, some of the chief elements of the Gothic style are identified. Some of these features are ornamental; some are structural; some, like the gargoyle, which acts as a drainpipe for rainwater, are both. All of them can be observed in the Gothic cathedrals in the pages that follow.

5

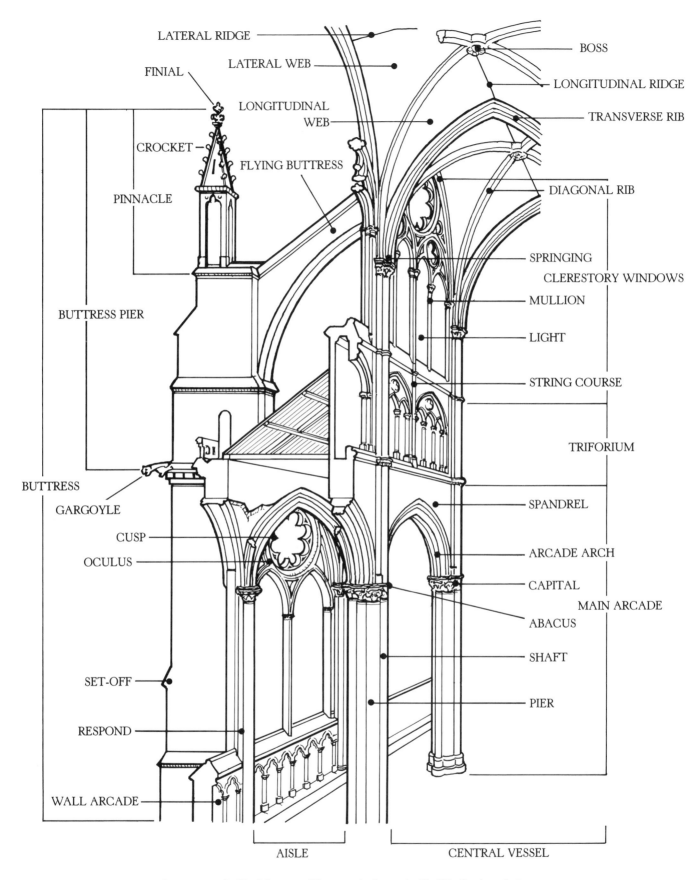

LATERAL RIDGE

BOSS

FINIAL

LATERAL WEB

LONGITUDINAL RIDGE

CROCKET

LONGITUDINAL
WEB

TRANSVERSE RIB

PINNACLE

FLYING BUTTRESS

DIAGONAL RIB

BUTTRESS PIER

SPRINGING

CLERESTORY WINDOWS

MULLION

LIGHT

STRING COURSE

TRIFORIUM

BUTTRESS

SPANDREL

GARGOYLE

CUSP

ARCADE ARCH

OCULUS

CAPITAL

MAIN ARCADE

ABACUS

SHAFT

SET-OFF

PIER

RESPOND

WALL ARCADE

AISLE

CENTRAL VESSEL

Structure of a Gothic nave. The nave is the main "hall" of a church: its central aisle leads away from the altar, its overhead space reaches to the highest point of the interior. Here is a diagram showing the chief elements, functional and ornamental, of a nave from the Gothic period. Shown also are some exterior features which lend either structural support or decoration to the cathedral.

Hagia Sophia, Istanbul, Turkey. Commissioned by the Byzantine emperor Justinian I, this cathedral, whose name is Greek for "Holy Wisdom," was built in the amazingly short period of five years (532–537 A.D.). Its architects, Anthemius of Tralles and Isidorus of Miletus, designed it as a seemingly precarious system of domes supporting one great dome on top which is 107 feet in diameter and 184 feet high. Though the central dome is a recurring feature in Byzantine architecture, the design of Hagia Sophia has never been imitated. The interior was once resplendent with the brilliant mosaics which also characterize Byzantine design. When Hagia Sophia was converted to a mosque in 1453, four minarets (Muslim prayer towers) were added.

Cordova Cathedral, Cordova, Spain. Originally built as a mosque between the years 784 and 786 A.D., the cathedral at Cordova (in Spanish, Córdoba) is one of the largest and most unusual cathedrals in Europe. Constructed in the highly versatile hypostyle manner (in which a roof simply rests on a formation of columns), the mosque was enlarged many times before its conversion to a Christian cathedral in 1236. The addition at that time of a 300-foot-high belfry, a cruciform choir and several chapels rendered "La Mezquita" (The Mosque), as it is still commonly called, even more gargantuan. Shown here is an interior perspective featuring the elaborate double-tiered horseshoe arches of the *capilla mayor,* or principal chapel.

Cathedral of Santa Maria del Fiore and Baptistery, Florence, Italy. The Romanesque baptistery, whose construction is dated at about 1000 A.D., is one of the oldest standing structures in Florence. It is three stories tall, made of white and green marble, and features the sculpted bronze doors (1403–1424) by Lorenzo Ghiberti which Michelangelo called "worthy of paradise." Begun in 1294, the cathedral is Gothic, but a distinct Tuscan Gothic. Making use of the high-quality marble quarried in the northern Italian region, Florentine builders naturally arrived at a style of Gothic different from that of northern Europe, where churches were generally built of limestone. The cathedral was mostly completed about 1420 when Filippo Brunelleschi, one of a series of architects to work on the Duomo, built its magnificent dome. The facade, however, was not put up until 1875.

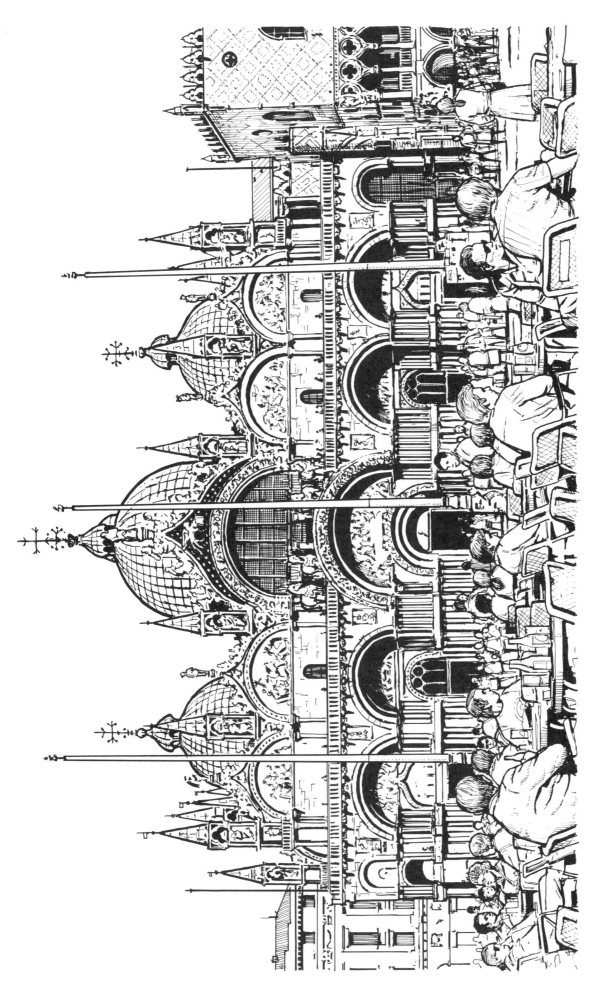

St. Mark's Cathedral, Venice, Italy. From about 840 until 1797, Venice was not only a city but a republic, an autonomous power which, in its prime, was the most formidable in the Mediterranean world. St. Mark's, mostly completed by 1073, is a testament to the worldly glories of Venetian civilization. Its five main arches are matched with five golden domes, and the entire structure is seething with sculpture and ornamental detail. At the high point of the facade, just below the central statue, is the winged lion, the national symbol of Venice; below that are four Greek horses from antiquity seized and brought from Constantinople by the Venetians. The cathedral, basically a mixture of Romanesque and Gothic styles, was enriched with new treasures on the return of Venetian expeditions for hundreds of years. The result is undefinable in international terms: it is an edifice uniquely Venetian.

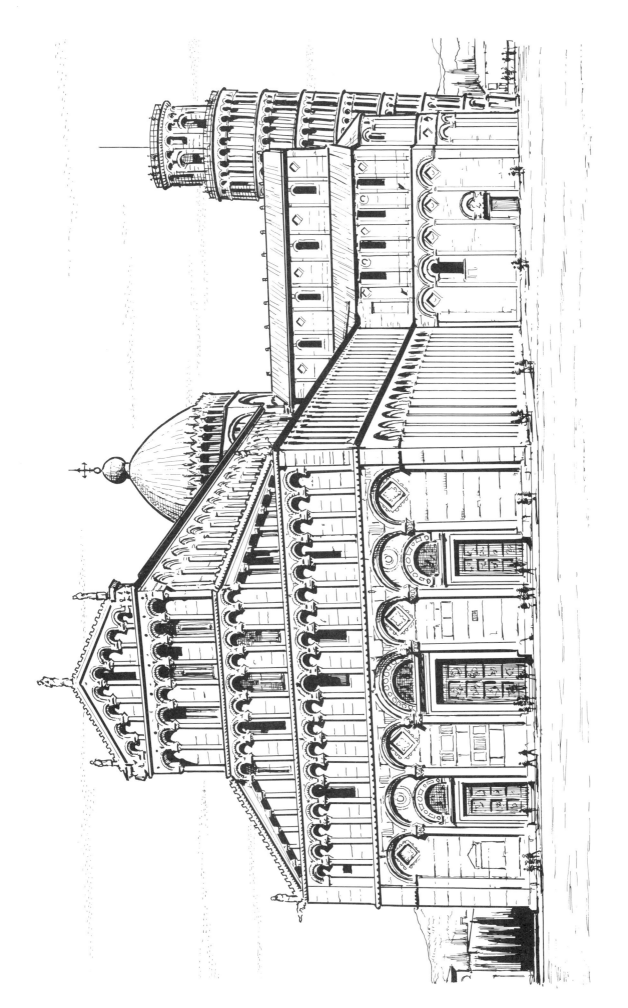

Piazza del Duomo, Cathedral and Leaning Tower, Pisa, Italy. Though much of it was under construction during the Gothic period, the cathedral compound at Pisa, which also includes a baptistery (not shown), retains a predominantly Romanesque look. The free-standing bell tower, the rounded arches and the profusion of columns all demonstrate the strong Classical influence. The 179-foot Leaning Tower (1174–1271), whose foundation settled unevenly, is about 16.5 feet out of perpendicular.

Cathedral of Notre Dame, Tournai, Belgium. Begun in 1066, this cathedral was conceived and largely executed in the elegant Flemish Romanesque style, with rounded arches and a relatively spare exterior. But as construction lasted well into the 12th century, the Gothic style, with its emphasis on detail and ornament, as well as its use of the flying buttress, also left its stamp on this church, particularly in the nave (in this picture to the left of the main towers).

Speyer Cathedral, Speyer, Germany. Somewhat similar in design to Tournai's Notre Dame, the cathedral at Speyer (1030–1065, remodeled 1082–1137) shows Germany's own somewhat conservative brand of Romanesque, clean, simple and austere. Speyer contains the tombs of eight German emperors and kings.

Canterbury Cathedral, Canterbury, England. On December 29, 1170 this cathedral was the scene of the murder of Thomas à Becket, Archbishop of Canterbury, by knights in the service of Henry II. The martyrdom of the well-known and powerful archbishop (he was canonized by Pope Alexander III in 1173) quickly made Canterbury the destination of the religious pilgrimages celebrated in Geoffrey Chaucer's *Canterbury Tales* (1387–1400). The building itself was repeatedly rebuilt; erected first 1070–1089, a choir was added to it 1175–1184 and the nave and towers were built as they appear today around 1374. The cathedral is mostly English Gothic (sometimes called English Perpendicular for its emphasis on vertical lines). Featured here are the vaulted ceiling and the elaborate composition of columns and arches making up the interior structure of the nave. In the English tradition, Canterbury has a central tower (235 feet) which rises from the altar-point, called a rood tower or *flèche*.

The abbey church of La Madeleine, Vézelay, France.
One of the most highly developed sculptural forms of the
Romanesque period was the carving of elaborate reliefs in
tympanums, the semicircular panels over church portals.

Shown here is the famous "Pentecost" tympanum (1125–
1135), on the portal of the narthex (vestibule), which shows
the Holy Spirit appearing to the Apostles.

St. Stephen's Cathedral, Vienna, Austria. Shown here is the beautifully carved pulpit (ca. 1500) of St. Stephen's. Though it was added long after the church was completed, this expressive piece is in harmony with the structure as a whole, whose surfaces, inside and out (exterior inset), are alive with elaborate carvings. The construction of St. Stephen's is unique in that, unlike other large cathedrals of the same period (12th–13th century), it has no clerestory (a highly set row of windows in the nave; see the diagram on page 5). The result is an imposing roof of seemingly exaggerated size.

Cathedral of the Assumption, Vladimir, Russia. Built in what is called the Kievo-Byzantine style between 1158 and 1189, the Cathedral of the Assumption displays a mixture of various styles including Byzantine and Romanesque. The overall look, however, is distinctly Russian. Though made of cut stone, its design is in the manner of the traditional Russian wooden church.

Cathedral of Notre Dame, Reims, France. Begun in 1210 and completed about 100 years later, the cathedral at Reims is known for its magnificent windows and the impressive statuary of its facade. Its design reflects a distinct trend within the Gothic style, in which ornamental detail, sculpture and the effects to be obtained from elaborate stained-glass windows received much more attention than grandness of scale. This sub-movement is called Rayonnant after the radiating tracery patterns of the rose window, a characteristic feature of these churches.

Amiens Cathedral, Amiens, France. This cathedral, which was begun in 1220, is one of the finest examples of the Rayonnant style. With its many spires, elaborate ornamental detail and great rose window, Amiens is one of the most breathtaking cathedrals in France. Particularly striking is the asymmetry of the facade (this asymmetry, which communicated a sublime mysteriousness, was an important characteristic of the Gothic, in France especially).

Cathedral of Saint-Etienne, Auxerre, France. Known for possessing some of the finest Gothic stained glass in Europe, Saint-Etienne, which was under construction from the 13th to the 16th centuries, also features exemplary ornamental sculpture. This "Green Man" foliate (or leaflike) motif graces a capital within the cathedral, and is a good example of the attention to detail that marked the Rayonnant.

Cathedral of Notre Dame, Strasbourg, France. Seen here at the end of one of Strasbourg's narrow streets, the facade of Notre Dame takes on a heightened dramatic intensity. It is not the worst perspective from which to view a great cathedral: such churches were designed to be impressive from any angle, even (perhaps *especially*) when partially obscured by other buildings. This church, begun around 1230, also has a single tower (not shown) which rises 455 feet over Strasbourg.

Westminster Abbey, London, England. Built and rebuilt many times, this church took on its present form largely between 1245, when Henry III began to refashion it in the Gothic manner, and the late 14th century, when the nave was completed; the towers, however, were not put up until 1745. The interior of Westminster Abbey is a veritable museum of tombs and memorials, the north transept containing memorials to British statesmen, and the south transept housing the famous Poet's Corner, where great English poets, such as Wordsworth and Tennyson, are buried.

Cologne Cathedral, Germany. Begun in 1248, work on this cathedral seemed to outlast interest in Gothic building: it was abandoned, uncompleted, in 1510, apparently owing to the new sensibility of the Renaissance, to which Gothic style was odious. Construction resumed in 1842, and in 1880 the cathedral was completed according to the original design. It is one of the grandest, if most anachronistic, cathedrals in Europe, measuring 470 feet long in the nave, 175 feet wide at the transept crossing, and its towers soaring 515 feet high.

Cathedral of Notre Dame, Paris, France. New developments in engineering made it possible for 12th-century architects to create much larger buildings. With the weight of the roof and walls distributed more widely by pointed arches and flying buttresses, churches could be taller and built over broader bases. This new way of building also introduced new decorative possibilities, including larger windows (most notably the rose window, the large round

window to be found in most churches of this period), soaring towers and the profusion of exterior decor, including statues and turrets. Begun in 1163, the sprawling cathedral of Notre Dame in Paris is one of the first and most awesome examples of Gothic architecture. Its nave is 427 feet long, its width at the transept crossing is 157 feet and the roof is 115 feet high.

Chartres Cathedral, France. Begun and completed within a period of 30 years, the 13th-century cathedral at Chartres is one of the purest surviving examples of Gothic architecture. Its relatively short period of construction—at a time when Gothic art was thriving—ensured that no other styles corrupted the original conception of the building. Situated in the Plain of Beauce, the granary of France, its towers are visible for miles. (Inset: column statues from the southwest doorway of the Portail Royal.)

Salisbury Cathedral, England. Built between 1263 and 1284, Salisbury is one of England's purest Gothic structures, and the only church of the period to be built by a single architect (whose name, however, is unrecorded). Its tower, the tallest in England, stands 404 feet high and is the home of the oldest working clock in England (1386). Salisbury Cathedral is 500 feet long at the nave, and 200 feet wide at the transept crossing. The traditional coat-of-arms of Salisbury (inset) features its patroness, St. Mary.

York Minster, England. York Minster was built over the sites of two older churches in the late 13th century. Its facade reflects the taste for highly decorated surfaces prevalent in England in the Late Gothic era. Also pictured is a carved stone (inset) from the 10th century, discovered in York Minster's crypt in 1969, which seems to depict the crucifixion.

Milan Cathedral, Italy. Like Santa Maria del Fiore in Florence, and several others in Italy, this church is nicknamed Il Duomo, or "the home (of God)." It was begun in 1386 and took five centuries to complete. Able to accommodate 20,000 people at a Mass, it is one of the largest cathedrals in Europe. The Rayonnant-like exterior, along with its myriad spires, turrets and finials, contains more than 3000 statues in its nooks. Though it is obviously a product of the Late Gothic (sometimes called Flamboyant Gothic), the cathedral at Milan is still somewhat reminiscent of its Romanesque ancestor in Pisa (see page 11).

29

Burgos Cathedral, Spain. Completed in 1567, this Late Gothic cathedral is in the Spanish Florid style and is almost overwhelmingly ornate. The bones of the Spanish hero Rodrigo Díaz de Vivar, or El Cid, are housed in this church.

Segovia Cathedral, Spain. Designed by Juan Gil de Ontañón and his son Rodrigo, the cathedral at Segovia (1525–1577) is another example of the Spanish Florid style. High above the elaborately carved altar, the curving, branching pattern of the vault ribs gives the interior of this cathedral an organic lushness. This particular style of vaulting is a distinctly Spanish development.

Cathedral of San Francisco, Lima, Peru. The first stone of this cathedral was laid by the conquistador Francisco Pizarro in 1535; the church was consecrated 90 years later. Spanish colonial builders in Peru benefited greatly from the highly skilled (albeit forced) labor of Inca stonemasons, who had themselves built impressive temples and whose artistic contributions in the area of stone-carving, mixed with that of Spanish craftsmen, gave rise to the uniquely South American *mestizo* style. This cathedral is in the spirit of the Baroque, a post-Renaissance movement that restored Classical refinement and symmetry to architecture. The Spanish colonial churches of this period are typically austere and spare of ornament.

St. Basil's Cathedral, Moscow, Russia. Named for a Moscow beggar-saint, St. Basil's is composed of a central church surrounded by nine smaller churches. Built 1555–1560 by Ivan the Terrible to commemorate a military victory over the Tartars, the design of St. Basil's, by Russian architects Posnik and Barma, has nothing to do with any of the contemporary international trends in building, and maintains a distinct, highly colorful, medieval Russian flavor.

St. Peter's Basilica, Rome, Italy. St. Peter's is the largest church in the Christian world and the seat of the Pope. Built over the grave of the apostle Peter, it was first consecrated in 326 A.D. Since then it has undergone a great many changes under a succession of architects, notably among them Donato Bramante who designed the original ground plan, and Michelangelo Buonarroti who, after 1547, largely shaped the Basilica as we know it today. It is 615 feet long in

the nave, 450 feet wide at the transept and the dome, 138 feet in diameter, is 404 feet high. The facade was finished in 1607 and St. Peter's was reconsecrated in 1626. Strictly speaking, St. Peter's is not a cathedral, since the seat of the Pope as bishop of Rome is San Giovanni in Laterano. Towering above the altar (inset) is the famous gilt bronze baldachin, or canopy, designed for St. Peter's by Gian Lorenzo Bernini.

Cathedral of Cuzco, Peru. Built in 1654 on the site of its predecessor of 1598, this Peruvian church, like the one in Lima (see page 32), is in the Spanish Baroque style. When Cuzco, the ancient Inca capital of Peru, was almost completely destroyed by an earthquake in 1650, the entire city was rebuilt in that then-current style.

Cathedral and Sagrario Metropolitano, Mexico City, Mexico. This complex, which includes the cathedral (left) and the Sagrario (right), was begun in 1563 during the reign of Philip II of Spain. The Baroque conception of the church is evident, but as it was not completed until 1813 it shows a blend of styles. One of the most striking features of the complex is the facade of the Sagrario (or shrine), which was built 1749-1768 by architect Lorenzo Rodríguez. Its lavish, tapestrylike carved stone and tapering, pyramidal pilasters (*estípites*) were trend-setting in Spanish colonial church building.

St. Paul's Cathedral, London, England. St. Paul's is considered the masterpiece of the great London architect Sir Christopher Wren (1632–1723). Built between 1675 and 1723, it is one of more than 50 churches Wren rebuilt after the Great Fire of 1666. In St. Paul's, the architect blended features of the contemporary Baroque movement (the use of double columns and elegant, symmetrical towers) with elements of Classical architecture (the great dome, the triangular pediment of the facade). Wren is certainly one of history's most influential architects. St. Paul's is 515 long, 227.5 feet wide across the transepts, and the dome, 112 feet in diameter, is 365 feet high.

St. Louis Cathedral, New Orleans, U.S.A. The original St. Louis, erected by French colonists around 1718, was destroyed in a hurricane; rebuilt in 1727, it was again destroyed (by fire) in 1788. The present cathedral was completed in 1794 and remodeled in 1851. A spare, elegant, colonial Baroque church, St. Louis rises out of the famous French Quarter in New Orleans and looks out across Jackson Square, whose centerpiece is an equestrian statue of Andrew Jackson, to the Mississippi River.

Notre Dame Basilica, Montréal, Canada. Designed by Irish architect James O'Donnell, this church, in the style of fortresslike churches in Normandy, was erected between 1823 and 1829. The towers, however, were not completed until 1843, 13 years after the death of the architect (who is buried under the church). The west tower (called "Persévé-rance") contains the famous 24,780-pound bell known as "Le Gros Bourdon" (the Fat Bumblebee); the east tower (called "Tempérance") has a ten-bell carillon. The statues on the facade represent the Virgin Mary, St. Joseph and St. John the Baptist.

St. Patrick's Cathedral, New York, U.S.A. This impressive church is a product of the Gothic Revival, a 19th-century movement in which architects attempted to recreate the sublime and haunting grandeur of the structures of the Middle Ages. Built between 1859 and 1879 by William Renwick, St. Patrick's belongs to the second phase of the U.S. Gothic Revival, in which architects abandoned the flamboyance and romanticism of the first phase for a more austere, historically correct approach. Reminiscent of the cathedrals at Reims and Cologne, St. Patrick's is one of Manhattan's architectural gems.

St. Mary's Cathedral, Sydney, Australia. This Gothic Revival church was executed in the English style, harking back to churches like Salisbury Cathedral (page 27). Designed by William Wardell, St. Mary's was begun in 1868 and completed, except for its two main towers, in 1928. Its nave is 347 feet long and 79 feet in width; the ceiling is 95 feet high.

Church of the Sagrada Familia, Barcelona, Spain. Designed by the great Art Nouveau architect Antonio Gaudí, the Sagrada Familia (Sacred Family) is one of the most unusual cathedrals in the world. Its organic, irregular lines, its seeming plasticity of form and the sensuous drama of its facade are all features of Gaudí's unique genius. Commissioned in 1883, the cathedral is still unfinished.

Cathedral of St. John the Divine, New York, U.S.A.
Begun in 1892 and continued in a variety of styles, including Romanesque and French Gothic, St. John's still lacks the two main towers originally planned for it. Though also incomplete in other respects (such as the stonework of the facade) it is a fully functioning church. It is also a church of staggering size: the nave is over 600 feet long and its ceiling is 124 feet high. Work continues on the cathedral today.

Washington Cathedral, Washington, D.C., U.S.A. Begun in 1907, this cathedral has been called an "American Westminster." Its official name is The Protestant Episcopal Cathedral of St. Peter and St. Paul, though it is more often referred to as Washington (or sometimes National) Cathedral. It covers 71,000 square feet, is 534 feet long and at the main tower is 215 feet high; the nave is 40 feet wide and 95 feet high. Situated on a wooded hill 400 feet above the capital city, this cathedral's imposing Gothic Revival bulk is put to optimal effect.

Coventry Cathedral, Coventry, England. The 14th-century cathedral originally on this site was all but completely ruined by bombing in World War II. Only the tower and sections of the walls were left standing. Beginning to rebuild the cathedral in 1954, architect Sir Basil Spence incorporated the remains of the old church into his contemporary design, designating the space within the ruined walls a "Garden of Remembrance." Queen Elizabeth II dedicated the foundation stone in 1956, and the cathedral was consecrated anew in 1962. Seen here are five of the ten 70-foot windows facing the altar (there are five on either side of the nave).

Cathedral of Brasília, Brazil. Built in 1956 by the great contemporary architect Oscar Niemeyer, this church is part of that architect's total design for the new capital city of Brazil. It is one of the most striking examples of modernist ideals brought to ecclesiastical architecture.

Metropolitan Cathedral of Christ the King and Liverpool Cathedral, Liverpool, England. Built between 1962 and 1967, the Catholic cathedral (in the foreground) is made of concrete, glass and aluminum. Its ultramodern design features a great conical roof with a pillar at the top ending in a circle of spires that represents the Crown of Thorns. The Anglican cathedral (in the distance) is made of red sandstone and is the largest Anglican church in England. Commissioned in 1904 by King Edward VII, this massive Gothic Revival edifice was completed in 1978.